SHORT CYCLES

Toho Publishing Chapbook Series I

Sam Fischer

TOHO
PUBLISHING

FIRST EDITION

Cover design by Josh Martin
Art by Sam Fischer
Original layout design by Andrés Cruciani

Editor: Clare Fentress
Series editor: Sean Hanrahan

ISBN 978-1-7336575-8-7 (paperback)

www.tohopub.com

Mom and Dad, Paul Prevou, Ms. Saladino, Tribe 12 2019 fellows, Emma Woodworth, Cassidy Fogg and Evan Dubchansky Julia Reeves, Alayna, Michael Angelo Smith, Zeke Zimmer, Tom Fischer, Brittany Sterner, Jane Fischer, Shoshana Gordon, Ben Rowles, Andrew Gordon, Collin Smith and Nina Finley, Josh Martin and Nikki Whitney, Nick Gross, Andrés Cruciani and Faina Ibragimova, Phil Dykhouse, Sean Hanrahan, Caroline Furr, Ben Saff, Hazel The Aura, Katrina Roberts, Thatcher Snyder, Enni (thanks for praying for me), and Clare Fentress, my incredible, understanding, keen-eyed, and supportive editor—thank you all for making this possible.

Contents

Three Meditations

Do Birds Dream of Falling

Home

Julia

Dream Chasing

David

Holding On and Letting Go

Three Meditations

At every moment let us picture it in our imagination in all its aspects. At the stumbling of a horse, the fall of a tile, the slightest pin prick. let us promptly chew on this: Well, what if it were death itself?

—Michel de Montaigne, from *How to Live* by Sarah Bakewell

I. The Pin Prick

Oh
It's a British voice inside your head,
sounding like an infinite echoing stewardess—
exhausted, honest, almost dead.
They say it probably won't hurt,
and you may not even notice really,
but look closer and there it is,
leaking: a teal globe at the
tip of your finger. You gaze
at it, opaque—seminal—all your
time and stupidity culminating
in a final cloudy underwhelmingly small
stupidity.
The room will be purple and
your skin will be pale and you'll find
yourself in a strip of aquamarine color
that narrows out from you.
But if you listen, you can hear the hush,
the shuffle, the scrape of voices:
the space between the iridescent scales
that form and reform memories—
and when the walls
of the only house you've
ever lived in fall away,
it carries you out,
in glitter and idiocy and buoyancy,
with you on your back thinking,
well, if this isn't the stupidest thing
but when those walls fall away,
somehow
it will carry you out.

II. The Stumbling of a Horse

If they hadn't—
if they'd not shot him on the track
he might have thought
that this could mean new life:
one to rest, to fatten, to notice age,
to go slow. To hold air in.
He would have deserved it—
had been worked hard enough,
had been kicked enough,
raced and heaved heavy
over bits, in blinders,
ribs in between stirrups,
reaching for inches of margins,
for air.

But they did shoot him.
And most people had already turned away,
to return to their living:
in houses,
in closets,
buses,
and stations.

There is a painful narrowness
to being held between things.

II. The Stumbling of a Horse (Reprise)

The track is a riot.
A gun fires.
A gun fires.

III. The Fall of a Tile

Its time had come, I guess. Or, maybe its time had passed.
It had been a while. It's funny, you don't expect to see
your memories again; you expect they stay hidden,
where they've been, inside your head. This one, this
was a fish scale, although it's not really one now,
being just a broken piece of glass on the ground.
A more broken piece, I guess. I had stuck it up there,
in the plaster, when I was ten; I hadn't thought of it
till I walked by and saw them tearing my school down.
But even so it took me right back; it was a good time
in her class and I guess it stuck with me, somewhere.
She cared. Even the one time after I punched that kid,
she never stuttered, or left the spot where she was,
right next to me. She had cool, small hands and would
lightly hold one of mine on my shaking way to saying
I'm sorry, and she didn't even have to move or say
nothing to bring me in and calm me down, and I did—
and maybe that's it. Maybe that's why I looked down,
felt so damn bad and empty about that glass fish
broken on the floor with the rest of it: it was like
some totem giving one clear moment to you out of a
sea of feeling and not remembering, and then,
you watch it pass away right in front of you,
right as it makes you remember. Seeing it broken
was watching that moment rise out of the glass
and realizing that it didn't have anything to hold it.
Wondering, if it broke, if I wasn't broken, and,
if it held that spirit of memory, if I could hold it too.
So I put pieces in my pocket. To keep it, against
forgetting. Things like that. Things like that, they
keep me up at night, trying to glue those little pieces
of glittering glass together, just trying to hold on
to something, I guess. Just trying to hold on.

Do Birds Dream of Falling

1

Do birds dream of falling?
Wings held close to silver bodies
shaped like lead fishing weights?

Their shape like the space
between the pinkies
of two cupped hands

that close when something
is given into them

moving one
over the other

fluttering
like a valve
in the chamber
of the heart

of some falling bird.

2

It must
be
hard

to always
have
to move
your
wings

just

to stay
alive

3

Joyous
          joyful day

raise higher
          my eyes
                    into that

              blue sky

Let
          my spirit be
              that pinwheeling
                  chit chattering
                      swallow!
Oh
        I would be no different
                  than he

        only further aloft

              with those hollow bones
                      that ring
                  with song

Home

Breaking Camp

When   we
dumped   our
boots   out
after   we
walked   through
the   creek
and   took
our   socks
off   like
wet   casts
wet   suits
and   painters
tape   (pulled
in   one
piece)   you
held   up
a   pebble
and   asked
me   how
the   weight
of   something
so   small
could   make
you   feel
so   at

          home

Laughing Inhale Inhale Laughing

Laughing inhale inhale laughing
lentils jumping august roiling
stovetop boil coil boil
that that graceful wonder
that that lentils dance
the warmth of cheeks of hands of friends
oh my friends what beautiful gradient we have
from laughing about something to just
laughing because we laughing
yes yes yes to the joy of a thing
turning into
the joy of just having joy
in the first place
yes to the warmth of hands
yes to the warmth of friends
yes to the warmth of lentils dancing in the pan

Julia

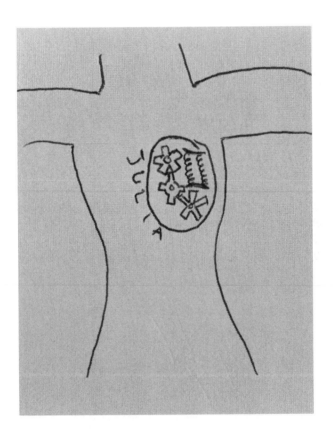

A Nice Slow Poem

A nice slow poem
about descending
into the night

about the rain falling
the sycamore trees
the hoodies' hoods
that drape over the back of the seats
about this trolley
and everyone in it turned
to the window.

Holy is the aisle
and the space
therein, the empty center
from which
we lean away
toward raindrops sliding
toward headphones nestled in.

Yes,
when I'm ready,
I blink
and finally
everything
has turned upside down.

And descending
down through the ceiling
into the rose and deepening
coals

of the night
I turn
and turn the sun over
until it becomes
the moon

and like watching rain,
I see those reds streak
into blues as I descend,
slowly singing,
about some girl
I met
at some
north country fair.

Biking to See You

The inlaid arch of the trolley tracks
in the asphalt I passed are traced
by the skating lights of trucks at night
and reflect like water by way of some long
ago metallurgy. I love you and so I've saddled

the bread I've made in the cleanest kitchen towels
I have and like the most holy thing in the world this
swaddled bread is full of tiny things that have passed
away that ate and lived and breathed to make pockets
of space so much bigger than themselves that they
gave their whole world what bakers call structure and
helped make that structure rise

and maybe that's something I can take solace in when
I remember the words that *the world is ending* that
we made space together and rather than collapsing
that space was structure and will be a home for
someone else's air and hope and in doing so
we made something bigger than us rise
and maybe that's something we can
take solace in when it's unwrapped
when the candles' light traces
the path for prayer when we
wait for God to join us in
the drawing darkness
and hold it like
we hold each other,
warm and thick,
with space
and
nothingness,

rising
like we are together
the most holy thing,
like this life is what it is,
which is holy, which is space
and warmth and possibility
and nothingness.

Emptiness and Confusion

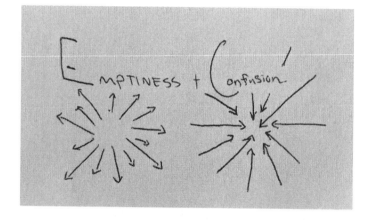

Velvet

I touched them
tentatively at first,
the shifting
gray colony
of midges
that had landed
on the tree.

The farmers
had been
burning
their fields,
so at first
I thought
they were ash
or moss

until eventually,
I put
my hand
up to them,
like a doctor listens
for a cough,
and when I looked
back at my palm,
the wind picked them off
until there was just
a gloss
of red pockmarks.

I know we think of time

as a horizontal line,
but I think of it as vertical,
and I am hunched some stories below
the feet of the boy with the bloody hand
and hovering some stories
above the head of the man
I will become,
who is running his hand
through the graying
hair of his wife,
thinking of
the sharp
red memories,
and how like ash it is,
these moving,
living
lives
we touch.

Barn Burning

We stood watching each other
and I have no understanding
why I write these things, why
I look at you and remember
what has never happened to me, why
when the roaring wind came
knocking across your window I
thought of how they kept the ground damp,
how our feet sank in like the dirt was sand,
the earth radiating the fire like the air, like
pain skating through a nerve.

On the next night, a wind
tore across the mountains
raising up the shouting of dogs
and when you got up to the window
between you and the black frame
was indigo and the smell of smoke
so when you lowered your head
the night seemed to fold you into your shoulders
and I remembered the words
this too is the heart of the world
that thumbprint of darkness
to which the air, cool and damp,
flows like an osmosis of smoke
and it turns
and turns
the whole world over.

Dream Chasing

Dream

Some dogs find out with another animal's
neck broke in their jaws and maybe they
taste blood on the back of their tongues and
realize they had something in wanting that's
dying in their mouths something makes them
go back and howl down into the den feet
splayed out dirt gathering beneath their nails
howling for the earth to give them the dream
they want to chase again

Chasing

I saw it when he was running, feet crushing
that small piece of air hovering above the
track,

chasing what I'm chasing what some men
chase fingers deep in pussy or fists putting
craters in their home gym's ceiling—lungs
bursting on held breath, brown eyes trying
to put a piece of hot air inside a breathing
deer so when he asked me how I did it
how I could hunt I didn't tell him what
he already knew, how some people are just
out here killing for when the feeling of
wanting something pushes them past the
thought of the thing itself and how that fills
them hot brimmed with the ring of the big
secret which is knowing that wanting stays
as long as that wanted thing stays
just out of reach

David

His Parents' Letters

*

His parents' letters were slowly shrinking and sliding from their tombstone to the ground. David's palm was damp with dirt and vegetation before he could read the diminishing font that brought up small anxieties from the cavities in their widely spaced serif letters and empty parentheticals.

When he got home, his knees were still wet from kneeling and his eyes were tired from squinting but he had to kneel and squint and crane his neck to make out his grain-sized mama and papa in their old Gap sweaters and Lauren Taylor cardigans who were standing on the table.

"What happened?" he asked them.

> "We wasted our youth on useless
> youthful calligraphy,
> big neon signs,
> spray paint,
> permanent markers,
> garish things with words like
> 'I was here' and 'plz fuck Me'."

David burned with embarrassment while his parents shrugged.

*

When they did pass away the funeral was austere. Even the tombstone was painted black in multiple thick coats of paint—in part, David hoped, so the shrinking white letters would stand out more at the bottom. Thankfully this variance was allowed, as the commissioner of their town had put very strict guidelines on the building of graves.

> *Chapter 155, Section 2, Article 4*
> *On the zoning and construction of graves*
>
> *C. Topstone and Headstone: Dig out a*
> *space before the headstone as long as the*
> *coffin requires. Place a long flat topstone*
> *over it, slanted 15 degrees. Meet the*
> *headstone slightly below the lip of the*
> *earth. Tilt the headstone away at 60*
> *degrees. On the long rock, run a sequence*
> *of asymptotically closing thin, thin, lines.*

In his letter to the son, the commissioner wrote:

> *I am sorry*
> *for your loss*

and on the back he continued:

> *Where this sequence of separated lines merge,*
> *these two stones meet. And they do meet:*

every single physical experience confirms it as real.

And they do not meet:
observation yields a gulf that,
upon further inspection,
widens until we behold a nothingness
that must always exist.

Despite our attempt to firm the gap with words,
symbols, and signs, it persists.
And yet, that same nothingness
conveys across it the warmth
of every experience
of touch.

*

When the funeral party departed, David waited, looking for dusk to fall. It was spring and the night was sweet with peony and honeysuckle that moved through the chain-link fences in the backyards beyond the graveyard. For a while he sat, waiting, in his black folding chair, the long sloping top rock leaning away from him. David let his fingers gently hold each other and watched the sinking white twilight behind the trees. The same thing must have been happening to the letters on the headstone, which had all but disappeared. He waited a little while longer for a sign but only smelled the peony and the honeysuckle and felt the breeze.

*

And the Light Breathes

Sometimes
he wakes up
and every cell is on fire
and it makes him think
of days in August
when his heavy body
stuck to the leather couch
and pain, heat, and light
fell on him
through closed
eyelids
today orange he'd tell himself
feeling for his heart
today purple
he'd say
some nights
but tonight David's mind went to a hospital instead
full of other people listening
to one another's heartbeats
and so is he
with someone he loves
who wakes up
and thinks of her friend
who just went in
and her cousin
who is pregnant again,
and with all the light breaths
of his lover
moving back and forth
over his chest
David thinks

God
what color day
is this

Taking the Wood Pulp Out

Taking the wood pulp out
from his chest David left
it next to the bedroom
desk on the gray slate
that rings out around the legs
and went to bed.

The paper was filled with salt
so in the morning
he could run the soft
lint-like pieces
through his fingers
and feel it dry and coarse
before refilling himself
so his body had something
inside to write its narrative on.

Buttoning up
he was thankful
for not making his body
hold wet paper
heavy with ink.

Wiping pale
salt stains from his hands
on the sides of his pants,
he thought of letting
all that ink evaporate
with the breeze.

The air that hit his bed and the slate

that makes the words of yesterday
disappear
was the same air that makes
the silk he wrapped
around the hole
in my chest dance
so gently.

We sometimes wonder,
would someone
mistake it
for a heart

Holding On and Letting Go

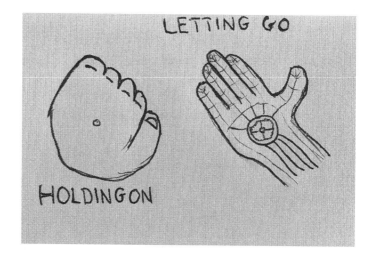

When the Flight Starts to Go Down

When the flight starts to go down
words like "no" and "can't" will drop
from above you

secure them by pulling them toward you:
ignoring the part of you
that can't accept what's going on
will not make that part of you go away;
secure it, and oxygen will soon begin to flow.

In the event that you must assume a brace position,
make room for the one thought
you wish you hadn't left behind
and find it placed beneath your seat.
It will inflate by breath,
and have a light,
and all such thoughts can be fastened;
so if you find yourself
alone in the water
know there is a thin cord you tied
keeping what you need close to you
and there is someone coming
who will find you.

Circles (Fred) ((Short Cycles))

Earth you swaying still surface you field of grain you
impenetrable cloud letting down the rain

it was you Fred driving the olive jeep you
hanging down like wisps of veils you in each hair

on the head of each grain moved by the same wind
that moves through the thin dark space where other

grain had been it had been days since we ate tracing
the circumference of a place like a plate watching the

light pass over Fred's face there's a tear in my eye that
makes the thin dark hard arms on the gold clock

before me sway its face so flat and metallic and bright
Fred your memorial was beautiful it was in the

portraits standing upright gold framed and tall with
backs backed in black velvet black like the suits

we wear Fred there's a light on your cheek in every
photo that takes me to the passenger seat and

both of us watching the rain Fred can you hear me
nothing passes away Fred everything I know

is everything and is contained and we are maybe just
a silent reformulation some bit of dust kicked up

by a passing gust or car or wave before returning
to the flat gold face on which we all must lie.

About the Poet

Sam Fischer lives and writes in Philadelphia. He majored in mathematics at Whitman College and also studied poetry under Katrina Roberts. Since then, he's worked as a mentor, tutor, coach, and data and evaluation specialist in the Philadelphia education sector. He is also a poetry editor at *Toho Journal*. His work has been published in the *Philadelphia Secret Admirer* and *Toho Journal*. He has at least four other chapbook-length manuscripts he'd like to publish (persona, erasure, haiku, and lyric poetry). He loves to create, analyze, think, love, express, and learn. He's excited to explore himself and his faith through poetry even more earnestly in the future and to put his poetry in conversation with others doing the same.

Reach out to him at SamFischerPoetry@gmail.com.

Made in the USA
Columbia, SC
25 February 2020

88386278R00026